I0760250

Grasslands
Maria Koran
EYEDISCOVER

Go to www.eyediscover.com and enter this book's unique code.

BOOK CODE

AVB43253

EYEDISCOVER brings you optic readalongs that support active learning.

Published by AV² by Weigl
350 5th Avenue, 59th Floor New York, NY 10118
Website: www.eyediscover.com

Copyright ©2020 AV² by Weigl
All rights reserved. No part of this publication may be reproduced, stored in a retrieval system, or transmitted in any form or by any means, electronic, mechanical, photocopying, recording, or otherwise, without the prior written permission of the publisher.

Library of Congress Cataloging-in-Publication Data available on request

ISBN 978-1-7911-0806-9 (hardcover)

Printed in Guangzhou, China
1 2 3 4 5 6 7 8 9 0 23 22 21 20 19

072019
121818

Project Coordinator: John Willis
Designer: Mandy Christiansen and Ana María Vidal

Weigl acknowledges Getty Images, iStock, and Minden Pictures as the primary image suppliers for this title.

EYEDISCOVER provides enriched content, optimized for tablet use, that supplements and complements this book. EYEDISCOVER books strive to create inspired learning and engage young minds in a total learning experience.

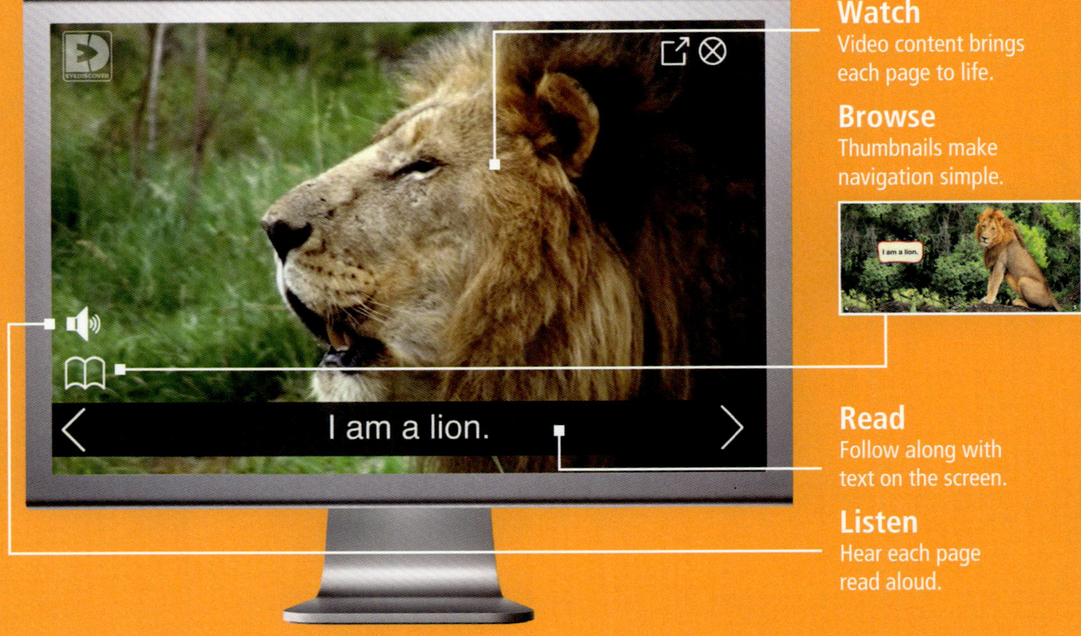

Your EYEDISCOVER Optic Readalongs come alive with...

Audio
Listen to the entire book read aloud.

Video
High resolution videos turn each spread into an optic readalong.

OPTIMIZED FOR

- ✓ TABLETS
- ✓ WHITEBOARDS
- ✓ COMPUTERS
- ✓ AND MUCH MORE!

In this book, you will learn about

- what they are
- where they are
- what lives there

and much more!

Grasslands are places where there is more grass than any other plants.

Some grasslands have hot summers and cold winters. Others are hot all year long.

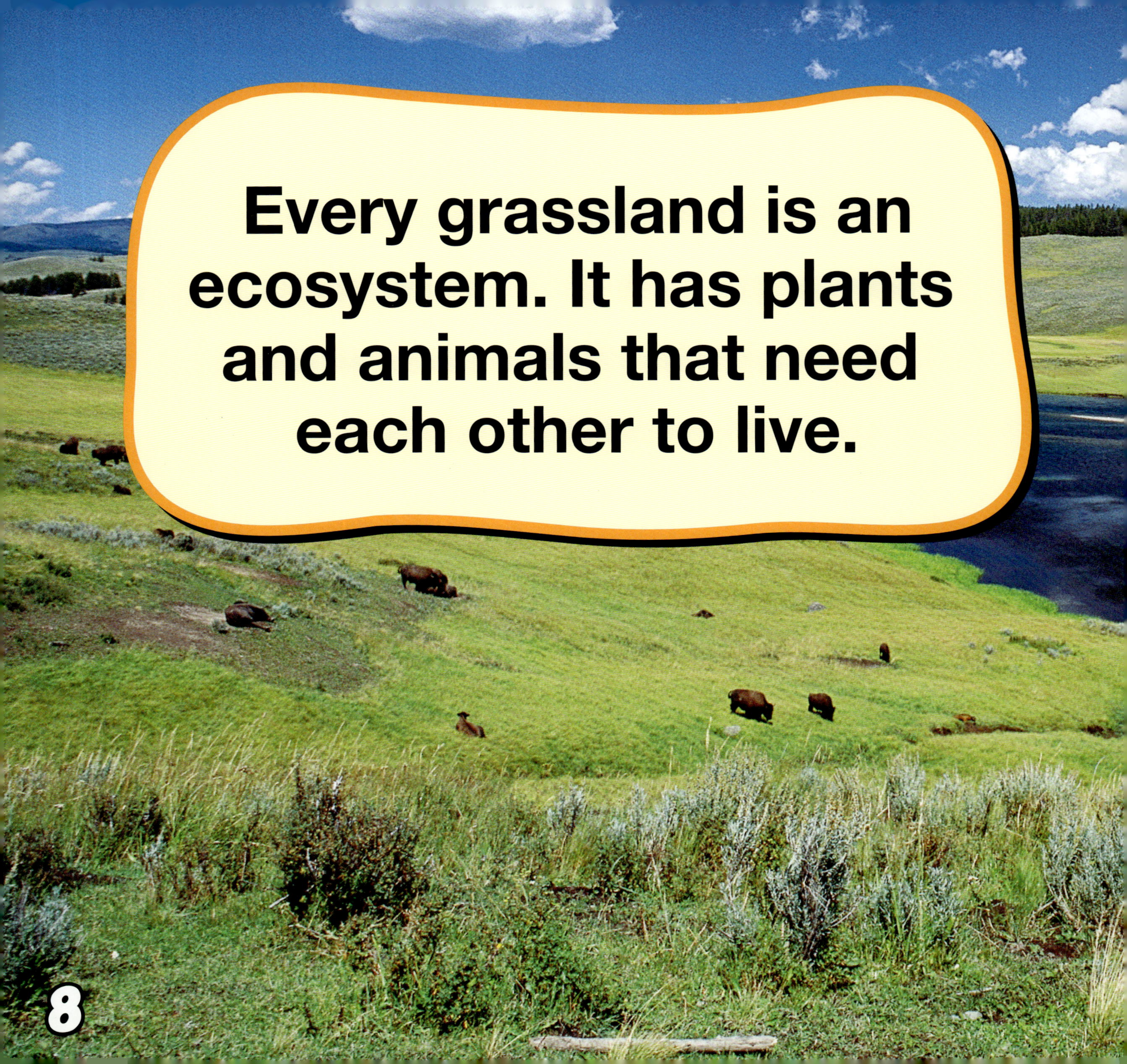

Every grassland is an ecosystem. It has plants and animals that need each other to live.

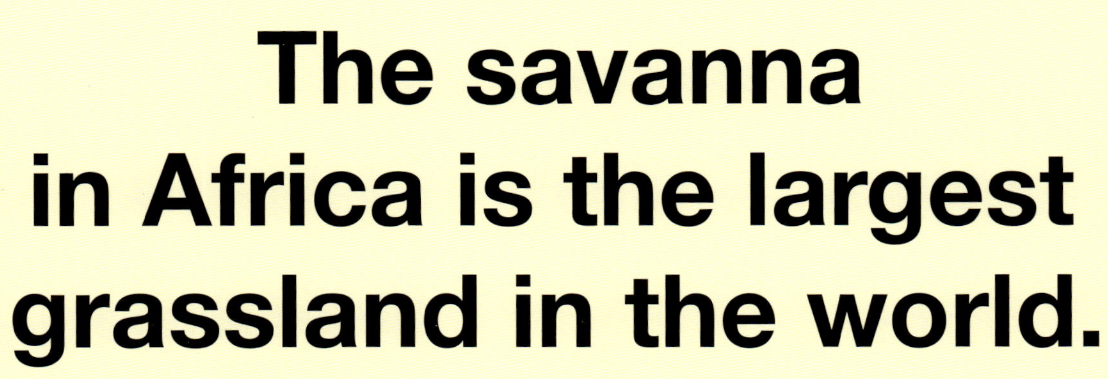

The savanna in Africa is the largest grassland in the world.

Oxpeckers help keep zebras in the savanna clean.

Many animals in the United States live in grasslands. They include wolves, coyotes, foxes, bison, and antelope.

Most grasslands today are used by farmers to grow crops or feed animals.

Very few natural grasslands are left today. The animals that once lived there need to find new homes.

Some grasslands are being replanted. This can help animals find new places to live.

The African savanna covers 5 million square miles. (13 million square kilometers)

There are 20 national grassland areas in the United States. The largest U.S. grassland is in North Dakota.

Grasslands do not get enough rain for forests to grow.

Most **grasslands** in **North America** are used for **farming.**

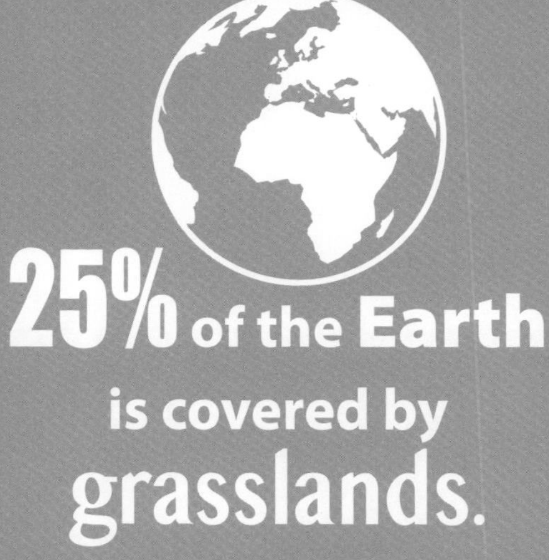

25% of the **Earth** is covered by grasslands.

Grasslands are also known as **prairies** or **steppes.**

Most grasslands have **two seasons**. They are the **growing** season and the **dormant** season.

KEY WORDS

Research has shown that as much as 65 percent of all written material published in English is made up of 300 words. These 300 words cannot be taught using pictures or learned by sounding them out. They must be recognized by sight. This book contains 47 common sight words to help young readers improve their reading fluency and comprehension. This book also teaches young readers several important content words, such as proper nouns. These words are paired with pictures to aid in learning and improve understanding.

Page	Sight Words First Appearance
4	any, are, is, more, other, places, plants, than, there, where
7	all, and, have, long, some, year
8	an, animals, each, every, has, it, live, need, that, to
10	in, the, world
13	help, keep
14	many, they
17	by, grow, most, or
18	few, find, homes, left, new, once, very
21	being, can, this

Page	Content Words First Appearance
4	grass, grasslands
7	summers, winters
8	ecosystem
10	Africa, savanna
13	oxpeckers, zebras
14	antelopes, bison, coyotes, foxes, United States, wolves
17	crops, farmers

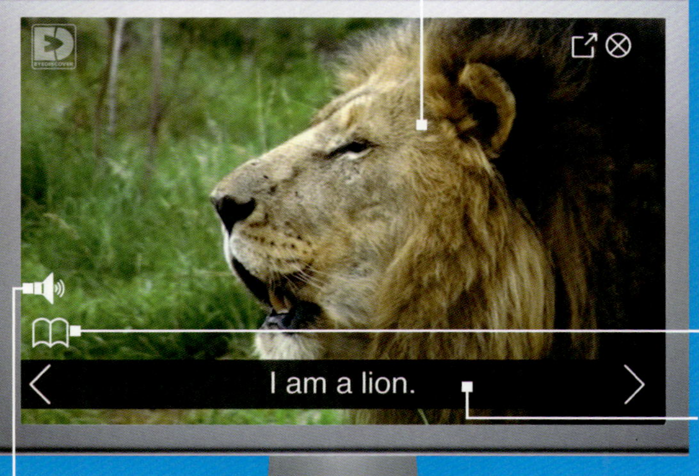

Watch
Video content brings each page to life.

Browse
Thumbnails make navigation simple.

Read
Follow along with text on the screen.

Listen
Hear each page read aloud.

Go to www.eyediscover.com and enter this book's unique code.

BOOK CODE

AVB43253